I0210783

BEYOND OPAQUE

Contemporary Poems

E. N. James

© Copyright 2024 – E. N. James

All rights reserved. Beyond Opaque - Contemporary Poems is protected by the copyright laws. No portion of this book may be stored electronically, transmitted, copied, reproduced, or reprinted for commercial gain or profit.

Reproduction in whole or part of this publication without express written consent from the author or the publisher is strictly prohibited.

Beyond Opaque

Contemporary Poems

Wrainword Wrush Press

New Zealand.

wrainword.wrush@outlook.com

enjames9@gmail.com

ISBN: 978-0-473-72243-2

Table of Poems

Walking by the Lake on a Placid Morning

Walking by the lake on a placid morning
Lapping the beauty of serene lake,
I beheld my perfect reflection looking at me.
Captivated by the still image and the still lake
I stood pondering life-reflections in nature.

Suddenly, my thoughts were disrupted;
A falling dew drop shattering the perfect image!
Broken image floating away ripple after ripple,
Distorted image quivering to regain unflawed;
Still stirred, perfect parted, I continued walking.

My musings were abruptly disrupted again,
A gust of wind flung dry leaves on the walkway!
Clean path messed by crackling, curly leaves,
Placid plundered, walking on crunchy carpet thinking,
How quickly things change in and around us!

In a whiff, another gust swiftly rolled up

The crackling, crunchy, carpet clearing the path,

Erasing all signs of disarray as if nothing had transpired a moment ago!

Revolving door of changes made me smile pensively –

Like nature, like life! Constantly moving, changing.

Reposing sun on the still lake nodded silently.

Gazing at the perfect reflection, I reflected:

How long will it take for the still to be stirred?

How long will it take for the perfect to be scarred?

A kingfisher responded by splashing the placid!

Fragmented sun dissipating in expanding ripples,

Distressed sun shivering to regain composure!

Life navigates amidst expected and unexpected,

Calm and chaos punting side by side in rhythmic-poise

Lending layers and facets to nature and life.

When all is placid there's no tune,

When all is rattled there's no melody,

Placid shattering elements of life

Make harmony of stillness sweeter,

Perfect and imperfect interfacing, surfacing insights of life.

Greeting Sun from Down-Below

Slipping into satin robe, I sailed to greet sun
Climbing behind the thicket of trees on hilltop.
Waving, smiling, I greeted him.
Beaming big, he said, "Hello, down-there!"

"Hello, down-there!"
Filling my heart with warmth and joy.
Bursting sun-shower soaking every cell
Making me an exploding verve of light!

I live a solitary life, in a solitary place,
Signalman's little cabin snuggly lodged
In the nook of a hill covered in vegetation,
Home to flying, fluttering, fumbling creatures.

In the valley lay unused, rusting railway track,
New track runs on opposite hill in front of
coniferous tangle
Whose restless fingers relentlessly casting
needle-nets
To trap and strap light-footed sunbeams.

It's magical to behold changing landscapes
From cabin suspended in midair.
Shifting seasons, morphing vegetation
Rendered by sprinting sun's inflections.

Greeting my friend every morning, my daily
ritual.
Some seasons I run up the hills waving good
morning,
Some seasons I run down to crumbling tracks,
Some seasons I wave standing on cabin-deck.

Sometimes, as I wave good morning to my
beaming friend,
A train comes puffing, shovelling black-smoke
on sunny face!
Covered in soot, sun blinking, coughing,
Spinning, swirling to shake off the soot!

Wish I had a hose to wash his darkened face.
It's hapless yet hilarious!
Train huffing, puffing soot on sunny face,
Darkening bright and warm countenance!

All I had to do; wait a couple of minutes

For the sun to climb higher,

Shake soot off his glowing face,

Wink and say; "Hello, down-there!"

When My Neurotransmitters Fire Me!

When my neurotransmitters fire me,

I'm out-of-loop, wandering clueless,

Skirting peripheral orbits trying to recall,

Why, suddenly all went blinking blank?

These days my neurotransmitters and I

Have an unusual relationship.

Sometimes we take different paths

Instead of walking together collegially.

I wonder, why they shut me out at times?

Why don't they honour the deal we made?

They work for me when I want, how I want.

These days they decide the terms of work!

When what is part of you,

And should work for you till 'you' shut down

Decide to abandon the contract at whim,

I shuffle blinking, thinking, scratching my head!

One of the unpleasant surprises of life is,

When you're walking the Sunset Boulevard,

Sometimes my neurotransmitters fire me;

Making me a sound-minded-dolt, dangling in
limbo!

Vexation of Simon the Sorcerer

Resounding reputation ran before him like
Santa's jingling bells!

Necromancer nonpareil of magical feats,

Wizard extraordinaire of all times

Sneezing Wizard of Oz to corn-flakes!

Towering Gulliver of illusions gigantic,

Awestruck people gaping open-mouthed

At the thundering, sparkling apparition

Floating in lightning-smoke-clouds!

Piercing black eyes set in ruby saucers,

Waxed, tapering moustache; polished, flowy
beard,

Sequined, silk turban flaunting pearl festoon,

Dazzling peacock cape performing incredible!

Brain bouncing,

Bone chilling,

Blood freezing,

Bravado of wizardry!

Timid and the lowly bowed low,
Lest they incur his baneful wrath,
Reduced to mice scurrying dark chimneys,
Chanting Confiteor for absolution!

God of his making, yearning adoration,
Cynosure, generously scattering delectables!
Candies and cupcakes; pearls and diamonds;
Crowd scrambling like crabs to grab.

Stuffing mouths, cramming pockets.
Drooling over stroke of fortune!
Candies and cupcakes melting snowflakes,
Pearls and diamonds draining droplets!

Magic not miracle,
Fading not permanent,
Illusion not real,
Fake not genuine.

Simon the Sorcerer,

Self-proclaimed god of wizardry,

Sweating hard to buy adoration,

Grappling to save draining reputation!

Toufee and Fudgg Tribal War

Thus, the folktale goes...
Separated by Happy Valley;
Stood Toufee and Fudgg Hills.
Toufee and Fudgg Tribes
Prided themselves as
Peace-loving, sweet-people.

But there was nothing
Peace-loving and sweet
When it came to neighbouring tribe.
They were thorny and bristly!
Vitriolic, vengeful,
War-mongering varmints.

Blinded by raging petulance
Nitwits even erected a sky-high
Net barriers to arrest
Butterflies, bees, and birds
Flying over to other side!

Rained fire over imaginary offences!

Once peace-loving, sweet-people
Turned hateful and bitter,
Fighting over trifles
Instead of resolving piffles prudently,
Over negotiation circles,
Refusing to see eye to eye.

Once thriving tribes
Destroying each other
Refusing to respect other's perspective,
Failing to carve alternative path to travel.
In time, Toufee Hills and Fudgg Hills
Became desolate wilderness!

Enlightened, surviving elderly
Pulled down silly net-barriers,
Walked down to Happy Valley
Planted white and pink myrtle saplings -
Pledge of reconciliation,
Token of peace and love.

Though the warring tribes are no more,

Toufee and Fudgg Hills are land of joy.

Preening in pink and white floral crowns

Rebirthed Happy Valley now, a Peace Cradle.

Fluttering birds, bees and butterflies voicing:

Once upon a time, tale of Toufee and Fudgg.

Transposing in Opaque and Beyond

Living in two realities,

Shuttling between seen and unseen.

Moving between sense and beyond sense,

Catching glimpses of felt not explained.

Beholding two realms - within and without,

Inside reflecting outside, outside reflecting inside.

Debating mind, vigilant conscience,

Placing wager on subliminal and abysmal.

Real and surreal contending,

Casting dice to choose opaque, transparent,

Or, to transpose in two realities,

Living beyond opaque.

Gathering from opaque and beyond,

Tangible and intangible perceptions,

Interception of seen and unseen,

Capturing realities felt not explained.

Charmer's Enchanting Charms

Imposter incarnates in many ways,

Radiant demeanour, enchanting charms,

Alluring, captivating.

Distract and deceive

Expertly played like a hand-of-cards,

Illusion of winning to bankrupt!

His coterie of distinguished henchmen

Manifest in many ways too,

Laudable enterprises to serve everyone,

Ventures in arts, science and scintillating
technology!

Once signed in, rabbit-hole plunges deeper,
becomes darker,

Bail with your life outcomes!

Baffled customers waking up too late,

Squirming to disentangle entangled lives!

How did seemed so good and useful

Become so pernicious and injurious?

Wasn't it created to help? Make life better?

Charlatans laughing, deception from inception!

Can you sell sugar lollies

By reporting its noxious effects in time?

Why would Liar's emissaries do good,

When the end game is to steal?

Divest, denude, devour the persuaded,

Amass and build empires on their graves!

Appearance may change to entice,

Names may change to make-believe it's new,

Treats may look different, inviting, appetizing,

Jingle may change to sell the new,

But the core; same intention all the way.

Death decorated in sparkling jingles!

Days Don't Linger

Days don't linger,
Time don't tarry,
Hours don't stall,
Moments don't stay.

Life on conveyor belt
Rising and falling,
Speeding and spilling,
Lost cannot be restored.

Life on carousel rotating,
Things added, things removed.
Seasons come, seasons go,
Giving some, taking some.

Lost cannot be retrieved,
Spilt cannot be gathered,
Lost seasons cannot be recouped,
Runoff life cannot be redeemed.

Course cannot be altered,
Ride cannot be reversed,
Racing cannot be halted,
Vanishing cannot be captured.

Days don't linger,
Time don't tarry,
Hours don't stall,
Moments don't stay.

Like Rose Among Thorns

Like rose among thorns,
Spreading sweet fragrance,
Declaring its presence unhesitatingly.

Sheltered from piercing thorns,
Protected from thorny tears,
Preserved from disfiguring scars.

Like rose among thorns
Blooming amidst adversities,
Proudly holding its head high.

Like rose among thorns
Speaking to many hearts,
There's a way midst of thorns.

Like rose among thorns,
Not losing purpose,
Unwaveringly expressing meaningful presence.

So, What Do You Do?

Social conversations invariably turn to,
"So, what do you do?"
I work for myself.
"Oh, what do you do?"
All that I want to do.
"Ooohhh, I see."

Ooohhh, you don't!
Why is it so distasteful
When you hear,
I work for myself,
I do what I want to do;
That may or may not generate money!

Why is it only acceptable or respectable
When you say, I work for...
Or I'm a professional, I...
Or I run a business that...
Why is it you're useful only if

You work within the established expected?

How's that you're less than, or unequal to,
When you work for yourself?
Solopreneur of a different kind,
Visionary doing what fulfills you,
What makes you happy,
Feel proud of what you do.

This may not be everyone's propensity,
The notion may be outside most.
There comes a time to dig within,
To know truly, who you are,
To know what you really meant to do
That brings joy and fulfillment.

So, what do you do?
I work for myself,
I do what I want to do,
It may not be typical, usual or customary.
What I do may or may not generate money,
But it's the essence and fulfillment of who I am.

Good Soul, Wasted Soul

Oh, soul, why are you so wasted?

Good soul, why are you so soiled?

Dear soul, can you be redeemed?

Sick soul, can you be healed?

Oh, dear soul, why are you so?

I was a pure soul once,

Then nature and nurture played on me.

Some continued to be whole,

Some like me broken and demented.

What's put on me tainted me, corrupted me.

Once good soul, now soiled soul.

People hate me, curse me,

Suppose souls like me are not worth it.

I was born a gift; now, I'm a bane.

Wish there was someone to pull me up!

Oh, poor soul,

Oh, dear soul,

You are deserving,

Don't give up, reach out,

There's one to help you.

Scavenging Rare Pearls of Destiny

Scavenging pearls in Pinctada Meadows,
Rummaging every nook and cranny,
Looking for precious, shiny drops of
Unique shapes and uncommon colours.

Some hiding, some sunning,
Picking gem-shells one by one
Dropping them into crochet-pouch
To read their lives, to know their stories.

Some silent, some loquacious,
Some fearful, some rattling,
Stories of many kinds,
Stories of every genre.

Fascinating, fearsome, joyous,
Heartbreaking, sad, unhappy,
Unbelievable, mysterious, baffling,
Courageous, mindboggling, triumphant.

Journey of many kinds,

Trials and struggles unworthy of life.

Sunny skies, twinkling nights,

Yearning of all souls.

Reflecting on stories told,

There's pain and struggle everywhere,

Pearls in seas, people on earth,

Pearls and pearl harvesters.

Journey of numerous kinds,

Life fascinating, life baffling!

Gazing at the precious pearls on my palm,

Feeling their tears of pain, and tears of joy,

Thanking each one for sharing their story,

Gently placing them on display velvet,

Unique pearls to continue unique journey,

Till each one is strung in gold.

"Procrastination" Partner in Crime

Later, later, later,
There's always tomorrow.
What's the hassle,
If you're not inclined today?

Times have changed,
Seasons have changed,
You're not ascending Sunrise Hill,
You're walking down Sunset Road.

Reminiscing the days of swift execution,
Jumping the queue in exuberance;
Meticulously organized in hundred ways.
Not a second late, a minute early!

"Procrastination" was my enemy!
Now, unwanted, shadowing partner!
Unwelcome caller dispensing unsolicited advice:
"Chill, there's always tomorrow."

"Relax, if your body doesn't oblige,

Why stress over insignificant delays?"

Take it easy, there's always tomorrow.

Did I say that? Yes, I did!

Wailing Cities, Weeping Villages

Wailing cities,
Weeping villages,
Howling winds,
Moaning Nature.

Spinning giant pinwheel,
Whirling smoky cyclone,
Cartwheeling thunderbolts,
Crackling electric storms.

Furious seas,
Raging deluge,
Shuddering land
Devouring living.

Thriving effaced;
Rotting swamps,
Putrid air,
Voice of wilderness.

Wailing cities,

Weeping villages,

Swarming scavengers,

Nature in mourning.

New day,

New season,

New reason,

Former expunged.

Nature rebirthing,

Summer buds peeking,

New colours springing,

New landscapes emerging.

New day of destiny,

New fragrance of destiny,

New walk of destiny,

New vision of destiny,

New dawn conquering,

Erstwhile disintegrating,

Higher pursuits overtaking,
New life celebrating.

Cycles of nature,
Cycles of life,
Some life erasing,
Some life birthing.

Impossible? I'm Possible!

Cracked sky, scattered stars,

Thorny path, wild winds.

Conniving invisibles hovering around,

Mocking eyes, profane chatter

Colluding to create "impossibles!"

Stifling life, squashing dreams,

Churning within, withering without,

Dismal horizon, whittling reason,

Grating voices reciting

The disjointed chorale!

Impossible, impossible, impossible!

Piling cold stones of "not-possibles",

Barricades, locks and chains,

Impeding movement, fettering progress,

Battling to make living impossible!

Courage erupting like a defiant-geyser,

Roaring boldness crushing intimidation,

Undaunted spirit squashing deterrents,

Hand of hope erasing "impossibles".

Possible, possible, I'm possible!

Outside it may look impossible,

Inside, it's always possible!

No prison can imprison the exploding spirit,

No darkness can darken the light within,

When it looks "Impossible"; I'm Possible!

Uncommon Brothers Rume and Tulul

Amazing acrobats, bouncing wrestlers,

Uncommon brothers Rume and Tulul.

There's nothing they wouldn't do to entertain
the patrons.

Run, jump; swing and hang,

Climb, roll; hiss and cackle,

They growl, they bark; they meow, they purr.

Uncommon brothers Rume and Tulul,

One wore brindled gray-white coat; other
brindled white-gray.

Bold, rascal Rume,

Stealthy, scallywag Tulul,

Together they played unsavory pranks,

And got out of pickle grinning like Cheshire cat!

Charmingly good looking rascally rogues,

This explains not being punished for the
mischiefs they wrought.

Keen hunters, snapping only bugs and beetles,

Enjoying slurpy "salmon and snail" gooey pies!

Though boisterously-rowdy at times, Rume and Tulul lovable goofs,

Known for friendly banter, and love of people.

Obnoxious Mad Rant

Once upon a time…
Obnoxious Mill was grinding, grinding,
Mocking birds crowing, crowing,
Devils in priest's collar,
Demons in nun's habit.

Blasphemous pitching
Topsy turvy, gnarled narratives.
Twisted eye, mangled angle,
Ladybugs are now dung beetles,
Dung beetles, ladybugs.

Devils in priest's collar,
Demons in nun's habit,
Planting confusion, growing mangled.
Mocking birds mocking, mocking,
Peacocks are pigeons; pigeons are peacocks.

Alchemists fantasies churning, churning,

Socrates, Plato, Aristotle morphing, morphing,

Mocking birds singing, singing,

It's hailing in the desert,

Cacophony is new symphony of the orchestra.

Trippers hoeing, hops into hollow guts

Brewing bubbles of insanity,

Longhaired Hercules in short-skirt conquering,
conquering,

News-bearers waving specious banners shouting:

Break-through of the century!

Mocking birds mocking, mocking,

Devils in priest's collar,

Demons in nun's habit,

Confused, feeble minds

Carrying new yarn to sell.

Perverse, peevish shrieking, shrieking,

Throwing tantrums, throttling normal,

Unhinged idiots making laws

Tricking to celebrate devious.

Mocking birds scoffing, scoffing.

Rancid narratives poisoning minds;

Mangled, tangled screaming:

Ladybugs are dung beetles,

Pigeons are peacocks,

Evolutionary morphology of the century!

Wizards in cassocks preaching, preaching,

Witches in cloaks presaging, presaging,

Avant-grade truth has many shades;

Surely, untruth is evolving truth!

Obnoxious Mill grinding, grinding …

Life Resuscitating Words

If your words weren't well of hope,
I'd have drowned in dry lake.

If your words weren't ray of light,
I'd have floundered in bright sunlight.

If your words weren't gentle showers,
I'd have searched for water in deluge.

If your words weren't tender whispers,
I'd have been deafened by soothing dulcet.

If your words weren't bread of life,
I'd have starved at banquet table.

If your words weren't water of life,
I'd have wilted by the burbling stream.

If your words weren't waves of courage,
I'd have drifted in ripples of fear.

If your words weren't rock of strength,
I'd have sunk in sand-puddles.

If your words weren't blanket of warmth,
I'd have shivered by the blazing bonfire.

If your words weren't rain of love,
I'd have dried-up in cascading river.

If your words weren't spread-of-kindness,
I'd have begged in teeming abundance.

If your words weren't promise of goodness,
I'd have wandered looking for meaning of life.

If your words weren't treasure of wisdom,
I'd have stumbled in the company of the Wise.

If your words weren't spring of joy,

I'd have sorrowed by the fountain of life.

If You weren't the sustaining providence,

My lamp would've blown-out in adverse winds.

Bold New Synthetic World

No cacophony, no incongruency,
No pollution, surgically clean.
Synthetic congruence, synthetic harmony,
Undesirable eliminated, scrubbed clean.

World denuded of organic nature,
No land pollution, no air pollution,
Synthetic world, synthetic humans,
Complementing habitat and habitants.

One ideology, one theme, one mind,
One voice flowing in one direction.
Magic of synthetic new world,
No dissonance of any measure.

Synthetic organics, synthetic inorganics,
Synthetic world of synthetic life.
Meticulously planned, perfectly tuned,
Conformed resonance, desired outcomes.

Anomalies scrupulously weeded.

Universal values, universal lifestyles,

Universal circuit servicing all.

Congruent, Bold New Synthetic World!

Conundrum of The Mismatched!

Sucked into a giant bubble floating haphazardly,

Seeing strange through iridescent fluid colours,

Balancing precariously lest the bubble should burst

In an attempt to sail away from the illogical,

Scribbling riddles of mismatched on my shirt-sleeve.

Willows sweeping sand-dunes,

Camel caravans on highway ninety-one,

Lightning conducting sizzling orchestra,

Piper piping on ghost ship,

People assiduously looking for evaporating self!

Silhouettes wrapped in shrouds

Stealthily creeping, slowly engulfing.

Shifty shadows hanging on,

Shuffling silently side by side!

Lingering shadows clinging to dwindling day.

Bubble tumbling like a Zorb ball,

Down the hill, over the fence.

Irised vision, nonplussed mind,

Train of stars surfing seas,

Trees on sky waving goodbye!

Sanity of Dislodged and Replanted

Dislodged and replanted,

Alien in an alien-soil,

Unfamiliar-one in unfamiliar surroundings,

Trying to stretch limbs and spread roots,

But shunned by native species as foreign!

Unable to grow fully, stunted.

Failing to reach full potential,

Petering self-worth, loosing identity.

Wandering purposefully,

As though on an urgent errand,

Rushing, smiling, waving,

Pretending all's well,

Feeling rejected, unwelcome.

Dislodged and replanted tree,

In an alien soil, trying to fit in.

Unfamiliar elements, uncongenial climate,

Striving to grow and blossom,

Trying hard to be like native species,

Yet the soil rejecting smiling graciously

Pretending all's well in appearance.

Imported as exotic to behold,

Dislodged and replanted,

In an alien-soil as alien,

Rendered redundant to function normally,

Retarded growth, suppressed true identity.

Dislodged and replanted,

Alien in an alien-soil,

Unfamiliar-one in unfamiliar surroundings,

Trying to stretch limbs and spread roots,

But shunned by natives as foreign!

Blistering Airport Rage

Outlander, outlander, outlander raged
The impetuous Yellow traveller
Glaring at the oblivious Green traveller
At the opposite check-out counter.
"Hey, you, go home. You, not welcome heah."

The Green traveller looked at the raging Yellow,
Calmly replied, thank you for reminding me,
Have a good day, God bless you.
"Listen you, I don't believe that."
Do you have to tell me that!

"This is my land; you, not welcome heah."
Nobody owns the earth, the skies and the
oceans,
It's for all humanity.
Enjoy it till you become a part of it,
Live and let live, for nothing is yours.

Peal of laughter!

Baffled bellicose, mumbling moronic babble
went on to board a flight

To Blue-Green land of white-hot-sands,

To enjoy the hospitality of many shades,

Under tall trees, sipping pick-me-up cordial!

We Are Meant to Pass Away!

Maze runners we are,

The moment we're born.

Running towards exit

To go where we've come from,

Where we are at home!

Maze runners we are,

Running with all we have,

Running as best as we can

To find reprieve we're looking for,

To lay down what's weighing us down.

Maze runners we are,

Encountering many scenarios,

Facing many situations.

Some speed us, some slow us,

Some seem never-ending corners!

Maze runners we are,

Running enchanted, running disenchanted,

Running into dead ends, running into puzzles,

Yet, making progress till time allotted runs out,

Exit imminent!

Maze runners we are

The moment we are born,

Running towards exit

From unpromising to promising,

To live without of mazes!

Fishing in the Sea-of-Life

With a small clutch of fish,

Tomaso pulled his little boat ashore

In an idyllic seaside village Marla.

This was his work; this was his life.

Boat load of happiness, no waves of worries,

Nothing he could ask for more than this.

Returning from fishing ritual one morning,

Tomaso saw an anchored gleaming yacht.

As he was pulling the boat on sand,

Swanky yacht owner approached him.

Looking at the meager catch, smirking wryly, asked;

"Is that all you caught?"

Sì Signore, that's all I need to catch.

Why not more? Asked the swanky tourist.

That's all I need to feed my family.

So, what do you do after this?

I go to market, sell some,

Take home some.

"Where do you live?"
We live by the sea not far from here,
My moglie Maria and our children.
"What do you in the afternoons?"
Rest awhile, play awhile,
Meet with amici.

Gilded tourist looked at the simple fisherman,
Pitying, asked, "Don't you want more?"
More? Why?
"To have better life."
Better life? How?
"Fish more, earn more."

And Signore?
"Buy a big boat, fish more,
More fish, more money.
Buy more boats, hire fishermen,
Build a fish plant,
Expand distribution."

Then what, Signore?

"Invest in real estate,

When you have money to burn,

Sell all for spill-over profit.

Upgrade from fish market to stock market!

Drink the pleasures of life!"

"Buy a seaside villa, sipping wine watch sunset,

Play golf with friends, sail with family,

Fish for fun!

Work hard, work more,

In twenty years, you're a multi-millionaire!

Living the dream!"

The simple fisherman smiled, saying,

Very well, Signore, I have it all here and now!

Why would I waste twenty years of my life

Torturing me, my family and my friends,

Chasing someone else's dream,

When I'm living my dream now?

"I suppose so",

Mumbled the gilded tourist reluctantly.

"Happiness and prosperity

Different kettle of fish

To different people." saying,

The swanky tourist waddled off to fish more.

Agenda: Homogenize to Amalgamate

Council of the Elites of Planet Proud

Closely observing their neighbours,

Planet of highly evolved Homo sapiens,

Agenda: Homogenize and Amalgamate.

Impressed Elites applauded vicariously

The creative impiety of the highly evolved to
control and rule.

Specially designed malware exploding like nukes,

Mushrooming spamdemic unleashing
impairment syndrome,

Stupendous fallout revolutionizing global-
climate.

Wickedly ingenious! Clamoured the power-
thirsty demented.

Let's try the first step of Homogenizing Therapy!

Deplatform the debating, prosecute the
protesting.

Elite Council will design the lives of the residents,

Fracture the unfractured, amalgamate the fractured!

Homogenized one Proud Planet of Megacephalus!

Iniquitously glamorous they chorused!

Hitch-Hiking Creatures of the Wild

Walking through the woods,

Inhaling luscious dawn fragrance,

Heart pumping exhilaration,

Body and soul throbbing life.

Supping sunlight elixir

I came home and shook myself.

Hitch-hiking creatures wild

Began to drop on white-tile floor!

Array of creatures of the Wild,

Big and small, odorous and odorless,

Colorful-ones and pale-ones,

Crawling, flying, hopping creatures!

Wondering, how they caught me unawares;

Why they hitched a ride home,

I gathered them to return to the Wild,

Afore, the slinky-ones become invisible!

Shewing wild-creatures where they belonged,

I was returning home;

Hopping, flying, bouncing wild thoughts

Hovered around trying to hitch a ride home!

Unsought thoughts trying to attach,

Just like creatures of the wild!

Some innocent, some impure,

Some dark, some honest.

Nevertheless, all weren't desired,

Harmless they may look and feel,

Still, they're unbidden parasites,

In time burrowing deep into mind and body.

Sooner you recognise and shake them off

Hitch-hiking creatures wild, better it is.

Complacency, indifference may cause
irreversible damage!

Hijacking body and mind, sabotaging life.

Quasimodo's Prayer

God of the Universe let me stand
And gaze at your brilliance.
I'm tired of life bent in pain,
Undo the knots, let me stand
Let me be whole again.

I'm not afraid to die,
But, let me live untethered,
Floating like clouds,
Flying like birds,
Before I mount the celestial sleigh.

God of the beginning and the end,
You granted Samson's last supplication,
Hear my prayer, answer me.
Axe the knots, erase the pain,
Let me charge like gale and lithe like breeze.

Too long have I carried the knots;

My eyes float in pain,

My breath fleets in groan,

Let me ramble like whistling winds,

Before I ramble over to golden pastures.

Chrysalis to Unrestrained

Never opening chrysalis,

Never alighting tomorrow,

Never ending yesterday,

Today is yesterday waiting for tomorrow.

Struggling in captivity,

Same dull existence,

Unsightly grubbiness,

Unchanging old, not arriving new.

Never ending previous,

Never cracking tomorrow,

Never ceasing night,

Never happening changes.

Imprisoned in one place,

Glued to sameness

Awaiting metamorphosis,

Taste of new identity.

Beautiful to come out,

Soar in freedom,

Dip in profusion,

Dabble in new life.

Cocoon may look beautiful and peaceful,

Struggle within is neither beautiful nor peaceful.

Hoping every day, tomorrow will be different,

Longing for new to emerge.

Cocoon may protect from harm and rain,

But prison is never a solution!

I feel like I'm trapped in a perpetual chrysalis,

Not emerging to rise to golden skies!

I want to break the mulberry shadows,

Unwind the silk and weave kaleidoscopic wings

To soar and sing; skip and leap

Siphoning ambrosia from gold goblets!

Illustrious Nothing!

Pretention, pretention, pretention,
Fairytale characters,
Big talk, loud laughter.
Guise, guise, guise,
Mere sputtering spume!

Character, education, career,
Looks, charm, persona,
Enviable, desirable, covetable,
Behind the façade,
Illustrious nothing

Like a million-dollar house
Flaunting impressive appearance,
A lighted match reducing it to cinders,
Behind the paint,
Illustrious nothing!

Life behind smooth plaster,

Much the same for most,

Travail, slog, grind.

Everyday praying for a break-through,

Expecting miracle to erase the humdrum.

Stuck between here and up,

Caught in the grind of open prison.

Choices without yield,

Actions without results,

Illustrious nothing!

Illusion of moving forward,

Feeling of making it happen,

While running the same mill

Grinding the same meal.

Illustrious nothing!

Actors acting impeccably,

Day after day, year after year,

Wearing entertaining costumes,

Scintillating, glamorous roles,

Mesmerizing fairytale!

Behind the glorious curtains,
Same woes and foes,
Half written chapters, incomplete stories,
Charmless fairytales,
Illustrious nothing!

Life without snags and snaps,
Singing like nightingales,
Dancing like flamingos eluding most.
Coach happily-ever-after not alighting,
Cruise-enthralling sailing to oblivion!

Riding on flat tyres,
Running three-legged race,
Balancing on tight-rope,
Juggling empty cans,
Tinsel models of tinsel stage.

When the show is over,
Hobbling out emotions spent,

Looking for something fizzy,

Instant boosters to charge batteries.

Pumped, poufs for the next show!

Walking in half-real, half-theatre,

Clutching spinning spindle,

Crooked wheel of daily grind,

Chanting chores like rosary,

Wishing for prayers to appear!

Expecting miracles to walk through

The hallowed portals of dreams.

When daydream is disrobed,

Quixotic grandiloquence, mere froth,

Illustrious Nothing!

CONSPIRACY! Slay the Lion!

CONSPIRACY! WOOLGATHERING!
Cackled the old Jackal.
Why should Lion be
The King of the Jungle?
Why shouldn't I be the King?
I can do better than him!
Foamed the Jackal squinting his eyes,
Steadying his rickety legs on the podium.
His rogue cronies cheered, shouting:
You'll do very well Sir, and we too!

In a bid to win by hook or crook,
Jackal launched his shady campaign
Against the reigning monarch
In the shadows of the Jungle!
Tables laid with meats and treats
Stolen from the farmers adjacent,
Jackal tempted the gathering.
No hunting, no gathering, no foraging,

My benefactors and I will attend to

Unhindered, plentiful supply for all.

What about the yonder wanderers?

Yonder wanderers threat to us?

Piped the concerned deer.

What wanderers?

It's a disinformation!

One of the many propagandas

Floated by Lion King followers.

CONSPIRACY! Cackled the Jackal narrowing his eyes,

Steadying his buckling, rickety legs,

Mumbling, swearing, adjusting his hoody.

My law enforcing, peace keeping

Hyena Squad will eliminate all threats!

The rogue squad slobbered agreement

Concealing treacherous intentions.

Again, the Jackal hissed, CONSPIRACY!

In a bid to pull the rug under Lion's feet.

When Jackal's supporters about to cheer,

Thunderous roar shook the Jungle!

Crowd scuttled furtively; conspirators melted into shadows.

To be continued …

What's Within You, Changes What's Around You

Breaking News...

It's getting darker and darker,

It's getting harder and harder,

It's suffocatingly dark!

News Flash...

Clouds of bleakness getting thicker and thicker,

Looming disaster closing in faster and faster,

It's getting unbearable!

Is there any hope?

Will things get better?

Will foreboding clouds clear?

Will life return to normal?

Will children play again?

Will the old laugh again?

Will the young dream again?

Will people have fun again?

When it gets dismally dark,

It's time to crossover to breaking new dawn.

Let your light illuminate the world around you,

Let your goodness touch those around you.

Breaking New...

Things are changing, changing,

News flash...

Things are getting brighter and brighter!

Multi-Dimensional, Multi-Chrome Life!

Skills, abilities, and talents,

Marvellously complex beings we are,

The path we travel is multi-dimensional.

Multi-faceted-beings functioning in

Multi-dimensional reality.

Skills, abilities, and talents

Feeding multi-faceted one true calling

Rather than just one path of action.

Life of branched dimensions -

Colorful, exciting and challenging.

Like a spectacular wearable art,

Diverse materials creating one cohesive piece!

Life's manifold elements, textures and facets

Functioning effortlessly like a well-oiled engine

Leaving foot-prints in many dimensions.

If we were mono-dimensional, mono-faceted,

Racing in mono-lane, pursuing one intent,

Life would've been grey negative!

Soulless soliloquy sans supporting actors,

Playing mono-games sans challengers.

Mesmerising Fits of Momentary Monarchs

Puzzling it may seem

Self-appointed monarchs

Throwing fits to manipulate all.

Sheathed in ill-gotten fortune,

Foiling facts, floating fibs,

Revelling in impiety,

In a bid to chain multitudes.

Avatars of their making

Immortal in their audacity,

Steeped in debauchery,

Laying down precepts for all

Outside their clout to live by,

Reckoning they're above and beyond

The ordinances of other humans.

Convoluted trail of unmitigated evil

Coming home to roost in time,

Coiling round self-proclaimed monarchs,

Squeezing life-breath out.

Felonious gagging in their spew.

Redeemed, oppressed trampling pseudo
monarchs,

Reducing them to dust!

Sweeping Apocalyptic Undoing

Apocalyptic changes shuddering the earth,

Apocalyptic changes dismantling the earth,

Jaw-dropping disasters stripping the land,

Staggering disasters changing landscapes.

Cataclysmic changes shaking humanity,

Cataclysmic changes dismantling humankind

Jaw-dropping evil dissipating humanity,

Unrestrained calamities impacting the core of humankind.

Changing earth, changing humanity

Metamorphosed earth, transformed humankind.

Apocalyptic natural and unnatural occurrences

Birthing new perceptions of revenant life.

Shifters, Drifters and Seers

Tempest raging around me,
Reckless winds, hostile tides,
Give me strength, give me skill
To navigate the clouded sky,
Let not the shifters cause me to drift.

Give me strength, give me skill
To rise above the contrary tides,
Part the dark-clouds to see stars.
Let not my passion turn to apathy
To take the strides of lethargy.

Battle raging around me,
Let me not lose my goal-post
Amidst the commotion of focus-shifters,
Chatter confusing and misleading.
Let not shifting surroundings drift my purpose.

Parading Pompous Mummies

Tantalized by youthful-gloss,

Tempted by immortal-glory,

Fueled by grandeur-illusion,

Whipped by arrogant-vanity,

Crossing unholy boundaries

Toiling to furbish jowling,

Rushing furiously to arrest flaking.

Overawed by bewitching flawed-truth,

Pawning souls to buy youthful-immortality,

Bogged in muddled-present, fantasizing
conjured-tomorrow

Scorpions and snakes rattling cannibalistic
appetite.

Duplicitous fortune sweating to break transient.

Blind-to-reality, bleeding to snaffle the
forbidden,

Floundering painted mummies of mausoleum.

Inexplicable Urges of Pedantic Shrew

An inquisitive shrew scampered on stacks and
stacks of books,

Hobbled up and down the ladder scanning titles,

Dawdled through racks sniffing newspapers

Chirping in glee in the old Town Library.

The little shrew surmised he was different,

Born for a higher purpose than

Just foraging in the hedges and bushes

And rustling in and out of dark burrows.

He lived a cushy life in the old Town Library,

Hopping and leaping on the spiral staircase,

Swooshing down the wooden hand-rail,

Riffling through pages of books,

Browsing newspapers and periodicals,

Eavesdropping on whispering young and old.

He'd oodles of time to read and chew-over

Whatever he fancied without borrowing a page!

Once he developed a taste for reading,

Craving for knowledge consumed him.

Sniffing, sneezing, adjusting his bifocals,

Journeying the living pages gorging succulent words.

Laughing, crying, moaning, grunting,

Feasting on fiction, fantasy and fairytales,

Pausing, pondering, leaving footprints on

Physiology, psychology, philosophy and entomology.

Whenever his stomach rumbled louder than rumbling thunder,

He reluctantly trotted to adjacent schoolyard,

Nibbled delightful array of leftovers reciting poems.

Voracious consumption of knowledge triggered erudite-syndrome!

His ears flapped gawkily, his snout quivered fitfully,

His head was humming and drumming to download overload!

Poor little, perturbed soul seeking to unload

Bales and bales of stockpiled treasure.

One day as he was snoozing in sagacious-
pastures,

He woke up with an epiphany!

Yawning loudly, he squealed in delight,

For he had found his calling finally!

Squaring his slumped shoulders,

Dusting his furry coat, pulled up his trousers.

Whistling gleefully, adjusted bifocals on his
slopy-snout,

Walked out elegantly to educate moles and voles.

Smiling pleasantly, he stood on a tree-stump,

Coughed gently attracting attention,

Peering through bifocals, adjusting his bow-tie,

Lectured on dogmas of life.

Moles paused, puckered their noses, twitched
their whiskers,

Smelt the blithering, blathering silly, old fool.

Shaking their heads disapprovingly, paddled
away.

Unwelcomed pedantic shrew tottered seeking
voles.

Amused voles looked at him quizzically,

Sniggered at the blabbering buffoon.

One cheeky vole squawked:

"You need to see a shrink!"

Laughing hilariously, they capered away.

Puzzled old shrew wondered why skunk?

For he was deaf in one ear!

Suddenly, he saw a vision of hundreds and hundreds of rats!

Immediately, he scuttled to sewer tunnels,

Taking a deep breath, squaring his shoulders,

Shaking his furry-coat, pushing-up his sliding bifocals,

Twitching his whiskers, descended to shady-terrain!

Unhygienic, dark tunnels appalled him,

He wondered how rats could thrive in such dreadful climate!

As if struck by a lightning-bolt, pedantic shrew bolted up

Gasping for fresh air before he'd be drowned in congealed puddles!

Defeated, disillusioned, little pedantic shrew

Plodded back to the temple of illumination,

Buried himself in pages of realism and escapism.

Years later, when the librarian pulled out

A thick volume of *Bones of Existentialism;*

Out fell the mummified pedantic shrew!

In death he attained his calling!

Sealed in glass, grinning old bones alluding:
if I can, you can too.

Counsel of Crowther the Crow

It was a weepy, mopey, dumpy day,

Sky was grey, air was damp,

Woods, dark and glum.

Quivering birds puffed-up,

Shivering animals bristled-up.

Crother the crow hopped and hobbled,

Tottered and toddled restlessly,

Squinting and thinking, raking his brain;

How to dispel gloom?

How to fetch uplifting warmth?

Suddenly, a bizarre hunch hooked his bolting brain!

Hopping and crowing he called birds and animals,

Flapping and rasping he rattled his whim!

As if struck by a crashing thunder birds and animals shook,

Looked to the skies, opened their mouths wide,

And, screeched, howled, roared, trumpeted,

Generating earsplitting, hair-raising,
cacophonous siren!

Alarmed black-clouds looked down in
trepidation.

Blaring siren of hollering animals and birds

Hit their sullen faces like a lightning-bolt!

Bewildered, scared, they hurriedly rolled away

To escape the unheard-of disaster befalling
them!

Instantly, light and warmth rushed in,

Weepy, mopey, gloomy sky turned bright and
cheerful.

Woody dwellers lifted their voices again in joy!

Thanked Crowther the crow for his brilliant,

Downside-up, left-side-right, wild idea;

And, named him the official woody counsellor!

Preening in pride, Crowther crow pulled out his
wooden erhu,

Fiddled gloriously, poser of the Vocal Woods!

Day Resting, Night Rising

Deep blue, deep purple, flaming fiery-sky,

Waning sun soaking in steamy sea,

Earth and skies merging and separating.

Clamour in the skies, clamour on earth,

Rustling, rumbling, grunting,

Buzzing, borrowing, scurrying,

Honks, calls and twitters.

Herds and flocks retiring,

Roosting wings flying home.

Droves of beasts seeking shelter,

Rising dust-haze glowing in fading light,

Enswathing hush descending on land.

Deep blue, deep purple, surging black swell,

Popping, splendour of the dusky-sky,

Luminous halo of earth's crown.

Gentle warble of the land,

Hushed garble of languid lull,

Muffled glow of distant village,

Chimney smoke melting into inky stream.

Soothing warmth of house-lamps,

Wafting aroma of sweet supper,

Silence knitted with soft voices.

Bedtime stories, drooping eyes,

Slumber tucked in warm blankets.

When one world sleeps another wakes up,

When one world folds its legs, another stretches
its arms

Unfurling sable tapestry of mystical air.

Hoots, chirps and clicks,

Howls, roars and screeches,

Sweeping silence spun with rising crescendo;

Burbling jungles, bustling forests,

Splashing waves, crashing waterfalls,

Midnight blooms, spectral flights,

Blinking beacons, silent sails,

Whistling winds, winking luminaries,

Night prowl of reposing world.

Vanishing in Vanity Fair

Woes and vanities jiving together,

Perishing, pettish jazzing illusion,

Transient breath smoking ambrosia,

Cities of steel on faltering earth

Fortified caverns for forever-living.

Sinkholes swallowing fortified,

Velvet manors, feather castles,

Blowing in galloping winds,

Growling earth belching buried vaults,

Genies running from magic lamps.

Enchanted, fortified falling apart,

Body of dust crumbling in vanity-fair.

Forever-living on the wrong-side of heaven laid
bare.

Woes and vanities jiving together,

Perishing, pettish jazzing illusion.

Splendiferous Spring Flamboyance

Bursting blossoms splashing colours,
Sumptuous fragrance, mellifluous melodies,
Euphoric butterflies, rapturous birds.
Nature putting forth spell-binding show
For audience of many genres.

Silver-blue, peachy-pink, sunny sky,
Shimmering silver, aquamarine-emerald sea.
Bubbling, fizzy champagne waves,
Spilling over scuttling sand-creatures;
Seabirds swaying on blissful swells.

Whirling wind tickling leaves to laughter,
Giggling branches sprinkling petals of delight.
Nature exploding in extravagant colours of joy,
Embracing fans in swirls of cheerful fragrance
Bringing merriment to souls, dance to feet.

Parading in paradisiacal-feathers,

Birds chirping, trilling, twirling,

Pompously strutting in embellished nests.

Beasts of wilderness in bright, shiny coats

Celebrating the thrills of mirthful Spring.

Hills, valleys and meadows in vivid mantles,

Suburbs and gardens in lavish blooms.

Spring in their steps,

Anticipation in breath,

People rising to greet radiant Spring

Like butterflies composing to tear cocoons

To glide in sunshine, swim in nectar lakes.

People bursting with renewed hope,

Shedding frozen and withered,

To gather new aspiration-blooms.

Year after year Spring ushering hope to dying,

Resurrection to dispirited languishing.

Splendiferous Spring swaddling all in revival -

New life, new dreams, new aspirations,

Draping bleak and bare in vibrant fusion.

Artist's Niggle

Visioning, forming, contouring,

Texturing, curing, polishing.

Hours, days and months spent,

Fashioning uniquely exquisite.

Niggle-worm throwing guilt-bombs –

"Waste of time,

Waste of time.

You do nothing much,

You don't really work."

But I'm a sculptor, I sculpt.

Visioning, priming, sketching,

Coupling colours, painting, layering,

Musing, labouring in silence to birth peerless.

Hours, days, weeks slipping by,

Niggle-worm throwing guilt-bombs –

"Waste of time,

Waste of time.

You do nothing much,

You don't really work."

But I'm an artist, I paint pictures.

Visioning, rehearsing, juggling words,

Themes and tunes, rhymes and rhythms,

Writing, rewriting, reflecting.

Days and weeks spent in crafting conceived invisible.

Niggle-worm throwing guilt-bombs –

"Waste of time,

Waste of time.

You do nothing much,

You don't really work."

But I'm a poet, I write poems.

Muse stepping in stamping niggle-worm.

"Don't feel guilty,

Ignore niggle-worm's accusations.

You are a creator,

You are born to create inspirations

That touch the hearts and lives of many

To influence, inspire, uplift when downcast.

This is your purpose,

This is your work,

Time well spent."

Rose Glasses, Summer Reveries

Fervour of youth unstoppable, unconquerable,

Unquenchable like the burning midday sun!

Exuberance gushing like mountain river

Ploughing through impeding granites,

World lived through rose-coloured glasses.

Conquering spirit, visioning,

Coherently laid out frames of life

Like a perfectly conceived film.

No obstacle unsurmountable,

No hinderance cannot be mowed-down.

Rose-coloured glasses seeing life

Like a cascading waterfall,

Vision of unbroken flowing in harmony.

Youthful ardour proclaiming; I'll make it,

I'll live happily till night steals me away.

No gloom, no doom, no demise of dreams,

Conquering might of summer passion.

Heart and soul ascending higher and higher,

Vision of future growing bigger and bigger,

When unexpectedly, struck by shadows-of-
sorrow.

Brushing aside tears and ashes,

Running faster to catch-up,

Pumping more wind to wings of wishes.

Working purposefully, working relentlessly,

Riding strong; building beautiful,

Midst of progressing dream-scheme,

Waking up one day to plain-glass view,

World without rose-tint!

Bewilderment! What's happening?

Muted tones, subdued tunes!

Reflection of approaching autumn,

Sedate ambience; fading summer dazzle.

Time to reflect, recalibrate minutes-of-life.

Discernment revising blueprint,
Honouring, what really matters.

Glimpses of what's ahead,
The inevitable may unsettle some
When rose-colour glasses crack.
Some panic, some take it in their stride
Reconciling philosophically to changing theme.

Beauty of summer,
Beauty of autumn,
Beauty of winter
Cannot be compared,
Just pause and ponder.

Challenges of summer,
Challenges of autumn,
Challenges of winter,
Cannot be compared,
Just pause and choose.

When rose coloured glasses crack,
Spectrum appear less glamorous;
Life beckons to unfolding, unfamiliar.
It may present more valleys to some,
Meadowed hills to others.

More sunshine to some,
Rain and fog to others.
Still, when summer changes;
Autumn and winter could be
Lovely, warm and meaningful.

Unless, one chooses to wear
Grey glasses, glum boots;
Join whining, blue-choir,
Holding lamp to blighted patches,
Wearing somber cloaks!

Anchored Beyond Horizon

Anchored beyond horizon,
Hope tied to unseen,
Soul seeing things marvellous,
Eyes beholding just plain.

Anchored beyond horizon,
Hope tied to unseen,
Soul perched on tomorrow's brow
Watching unpacking dreams.

Anchored beyond horizon,
Hope tied to unseen,
Leaving mayhem behind,
Forecast cheerless and foreboding.

Anchored beyond horizon,
Hope tied to unseen,
Stepping out of tottering, sinking
To timeless sands of sanguine current.

Anchored beyond horizon,

Hope tied to unseen,

Unsightly disarray fading

Impeccable beyond unfolding.

Anchored beyond horizon,

Hope tied to unseen,

Unblemished tomorrows reaching out

To bequeath envisioned idyllic.

Seeking the Big-Light

Little-Light rose at the peep of dawn
With a fresh sparkle of expectation,
Flew to glowing speckled realm
Saying, today, surely, I'll meet Big-Light.

Then, I'll be infused with impartation,
I'll be refreshed, restored, renewed,
With revelation insight into knowing.
Transformed me will shine like a bright-light.

Every day at the peep of dawn,
Breathing the same prayer of expectation,
Litle-Light flew to the realm of mysteries
Where hope manifests in Big-Light's presence.

Little-Light went everyday seeking Big-Light
To be transformed to the likeness of the sought.
Every evenfall Little-Light returned home
Saying, tomorrow, surely, I'll find Big-Light.

Days dropped, years yellowed,

Little-Light growing dimmer and dimmer; slower
and slower,

Soaring to the realm of unfathomable mysteries

To touch Big-Light becoming uphill pursuit.

Stroking the fading, fraying cape,

Peering through dimming sight,

Spirit mounted Little-Light soaring to realms

Beyond sparkling, speckled.

Exuding undimmable hope,

Seeking the face of Big-Light,

To be restored to immutable,

To dwell in realms of dazzling dawns.

The Heart of Milford Sound

Draped in cold, misty mantle,

Breath rising like smoke from the censer,

Soul swathed in wonder and awe,

Entering the heart of Milford Sound.

Thick silence of frosty breeze,

Swish of furrowing, crisp-waters,

Mind frozen in silent surrender,

Feeling the heart of Milford Sound.

Pulsing deep-blue sapphire reservoir

Flanked by rippling, lush emerald forests,

Glacier crests sparkling like crown jewels,

Spellbinding magnificence of the fiords!

Rustling, slithering, slender cascades,

Thundering, roaring, majestic cataracts,

Shimmering, indigo ripples crusted in silver,

Glassy-eyed seals floating like velvet cushions.

Lofty peaks crowned in candescent clouds,

Trees hemmed in pearly, silk-haze,

Foliage fringed with crystal dew-beads,

Flapping feathers, paddling flippers.

Plonking tunes of prancing raindrops,

Bouncing strings of waterfall-rainbows,

Fluttering wreaths of dappling colours,

Banquet of pleasure, bowl of tranquillity.

Screaming beauty of the sanctuary,

Resounding voices of the Sound,

Coupling to birth rare silence,

Speechless transported to paradise.

Throbbing heart of Milford Sound,

Where earth and skies interlace,

Where soul takes flight to amaranthine,

Touching supernal on temporal.

Harp of my emotions playing,

Voice of my heart singing,

Head bowed in ineffable reverence,

Saluting the Creator of breathtaking!

Chisel and Mallet Ballet

Bowed in deep deliberation as in worship,
Beholding the unborn grandeur before it's born,
Rising to face the towering task
With a chisel and a mallet in hand.

Touching and feeling the rugged alabaster,
Leaning and listening, tunes of stone-cold face,
Pausing and musing, mulling murmuring notes,
Poising to harmonize and dance with the veiled.

Heart and soul flowing together,
Stroke by stroke, chip by chip
In tune with the resonating rhythm,
Uncovering the concealed wonder.

Stroke by stroke creating angles,
Tap by tap smoothing fringes,
Shaping ridges,
Softening edges.

Virtuoso, chisel by chisel unveiling the marvel,

Stroke by stroke unsealing the melodies.

Amazed gathering gazing in mute-wonder;

Stunning statue stirring hearts and souls.

Tinder-Fly Bower of Bliss

Let me bask in the bower of bliss,

Let me laze beneath swaying leaf-lattice

Watching tinder-flies bounce on leaves.

Fluttering breeze arranging and rearranging

Warm light-patterns on me and around me,

Displaying colorful, trellis webbing of light.

Radiant beams transforming earthly to heavenly,

Flowers glowing like vibrant, crystal chandeliers.

Fancy ascending with frolicking colours tranced
by tinder-shower,

Warm, sunny-scents kindling unknown inner
awakening,

Euphoric-bliss permeating body and soul,

Rapturous flying on timeless wings.

Tinder-sparks kissing somnambulant to life,

Raking dormant unknown to blazing flames,

Listless blurred coming to lucid vision,

Hidden making sense in blaring-bright.

Lighted bower opening brief windows into yonder,

Here and now, there and yonder merging into one.

Ecstasy of unseen-seen seizing the senses,

Soul thirsting for more supernal-natural

Concealed in open glades and bowers.

Tinder-flies frolicking in tinder-rays

Opening hidden windows of beyond

Unlocking mystique-marvels of every day.

The Known and the Unknown Fallen

Graves of unknown soldiers
Willing sacrificed life to preserve
People, freedom and their country.

Memorials to unknown heroes
Who laid down their lives for common good
Saving lives while losing their own.

Roadside memorials to known loved,
Casualties of speeding, intoxication and
cluttered concentration,
Not war but preventable snatching lives.

Sojourning Route 66

Arriving at Route 66 breathing gratitude,

Pondering contemplatively what might be ahead.

Peering as far as eyes could see the new,

Tossing aside deflecting matters

That sidetrack and hinder the journey.

Breathing deep the air of new walk,

Mind's eye surveying unfolding terrain.

Letting go irrelevant, picking up relevant

That gives foresight to the journey,

That brings meaning to new encounters.

Prospects of Route 66 – some new, some same.

Embracing worthwhile, felicitous,

Bypassing compelling wayside attractions

That arrest attention to sidetrack,

Walking steadily, walking intentionally.

Bestowing gifts to bless,

Gathering smiles and joys.

Journeying mindfully one day at a time,

Living contentedly with no strings attached,

Route 66 enabling till the turn of the next.

When even falls,

Night shall not overtake me,

I shall walk from glorious gloaming

To twinkling twilight,

And live in everlasting day.

Beyond Opaque

© Copyright 2024: E. N. James

www.ingramcontent.com/pod-product-compliance
Lightning Source LLC
Chambersburg PA
CBHW060413090426
42734CB00011B/2296